Way of the
Warrior

KNIGHTS
Warriors of the Middle Ages

Aileen Weintraub

HIGH
interest
books

Children's Press®
A Division of Scholastic Inc.
New York / Toronto / London / Auckland / Sydney
Mexico City / New Delhi / Hong Kong
Danbury, Connecticut

Book Design: Michael DeLisio and Elana Davidian
Contributing Editor: Matthew Pitt
Photo Credits: Cover © Darama/Corbis; pp. 5, 8, 19, 28, 32 © Bettmann/Corbis;
p. 6 © Christie's Images/Corbis; pp. 10, 31 © Archivo Iconografico, S.A./Corbis;
p. 14 © Hulton Archive; pp. 15, 16 © Hulton-Deutsch Collection/Corbis; p. 21 © Jim
Sugar/Corbis; p. 23 © Kevin Fleming/Corbis; p. 26 © Gianni Dagli Orti/Corbis;
p. 35 © Austrian Archives/Corbis; p. 36 © Michael St. Maur Sheil/Corbis;
p. 38 © Charles & Josette Lenars/Corbis; p. 41 © Patrick Ward/Corbis

Library of Congress Cataloging-in-Publication Data

Weintraub, Aileen, 1973–
    Knights : warriors of the Middle Ages / Aileen Weintraub.
    p. cm. — (Way of the warrior)
    Includes index.
    ISBN 0-516-25117-1 (lib. bdg.) — ISBN 0-516-25086-8 (pbk.)
    1. Knights and knighthood—History—Juvenile literature. 2. Civilization,
    Medieval
    Juvenile literature. I. Title. II. Series.

CR4513.W44 2005
940.1'088'355—dc22

                                                    2004003277

1 2 3 4 5 6 7 8 9 10 R 14 13 12 11 10 09 08 07 06 05

Contents

INTRODUCTION

Hundreds of soldiers gallop to a battlefield on strong, fearsome horses. The horses halt, then line up next to one another. Steam shoots out of their noses. Their riders wear gleaming armor that covers their entire bodies. They grip long, sharp poles called lances. They are warriors who are still reeling from the battle they won the day before. They are exhausted and thirsty. They feel like they're cooking inside their armor. These are the knights of the Middle Ages.

The enemy opens fire on the knights. Sharp arrows rain down. Most of the arrows miss. Some pierce the horses' hides. One horse is hit in the neck by an arrow. It rears up in shock and pain, flinging its rider to the ground.

The fallen knight slowly rises. As he gets to his feet, an enemy picks up the knight's lance and snaps it in two. The knight must resort to one-on-one combat. It is his first actual battle.

He has been training for this moment since he was seven years old. The knight reaches for the double-edged sword at his side and charges his foe. He can hardly see through the thin opening in his helmet. What he does see is his enemy falling to the ground. The knight's sword has found its mark. More enemies are just a few steps away. The knight refuses to retreat. He has been commanded by his lord and the church to fight on, no matter how long the battle rages.

Knights went into battle in many different types of armor and uniforms. The ones shown here date from the mid-1400s.

CHAPTER ONE

Beginning of the Knight

When people think of the Middle Ages, romantic images often flood their minds. Some people picture great feasts being thrown in a banquet hall. Others think of powerful kings and queens in their castles. The most exciting symbol of the Middle Ages, though, may be knights. These warriors are thought of as heroic figures. They are often pictured carrying shining swords and wearing coats of armor. Many people imagine them swooping in on horses to rescue damsels in distress.

The knights of the Middle Ages were trained killers. Knights were ready to fight at a moment's notice. They often slaughtered

In this 1901 painting, a young man is being knighted by a woman of royalty.

The knights of the Middle Ages were highly trained warriors. In the battle shown above, English knights defeated a French army of twenty-five thousand men.

those who didn't share their religious faith. Sometimes they kidnapped their enemies and demanded money for their release. Many knights looked to conquer villages and collect their treasures. Knights were brutal and heroic—at the same time.

First Knights

In the sixth century, with the Roman Empire in ruins, much of Europe was unguarded. Ruthless warriors invaded towns, riding horses to overpower their victims. Local warriors decided to battle back. They learned how to fight on horseback as well. These were the first knights. They were usually free peasants who simply wanted to defend their homes from attack. As they gained more success, their legend grew.

Soon, great leaders began to hear about these warriors' daring acts of bravery. Charlemagne, a powerful king and emperor, helped organize the knights. Charlemagne ruled most of western Europe in the eighth century. However, his kingdom came under attack, mostly by Saxons, a tribe from central Germany. Worried that the invaders threatened his rule, he formed a cavalry. A cavalry is a group of soldiers who fight on horseback.

This cavalry destroyed Charlemagne's enemies. Word of their deeds spread throughout Europe. The legend of knights began to grow.

Buying Peace of Mind

After Charlemagne's death in 814, his territory went into ruin. Roads and bridges crumbled. The government was too weak to protect its citizens. Thieves and bandits attacked towns at will.

Landowners lived in constant fear of invasion. They didn't have enough money to pay soldiers, but they desperately needed protection. To help themselves, they created a system called feudalism. Under feudalism, people were given land in exchange for goods or services. A king or lord who owned land would offer a portion of it to a knight and his family. In return, knights defended kings, lords, and their lands on the battlefield.

Keepers of the Faith

The Catholic Church took note of the knights' heroic feats. It was impressed by their bravery in battle. At the same time, knighthood made the church a little nervous. Some knights were stirring up trouble, and even attacking monks and priests. The church wrote a document called the "Truce of God." It asked knights not to fight from Thursday to Sunday. It ordered the warriors not to attack religious places. The church convinced knights to protect it, not harm it.

Charlemagne (seated) built a kingdom that included almost all of western and central Europe.

Priests and monks promised knights that their bravery would be rewarded. If the knights fought for the church, they would be guaranteed a place in heaven. Knights were ordered to draw their swords only against the enemies of the church.

FIGHTING WORDS

Sometimes knights were loyal to whoever offered the most money.

Crusades

Cooperation between knights and the church reached a high point during the Crusades. The Crusades were a series of wars fought between European Christians and Muslims living in areas near the Mediterranean Sea. The wars lasted from 1096 to 1270.

By the eighth century, Muslim forces had taken control of North Africa, the eastern Mediterranean, and most of Spain. In 1071, a group of Muslims called Seljuk Turks captured the city of Jerusalem in the Middle East. This city was a holy place for Christians throughout the world. The Seljuk Turks often robbed and beat Christians living in the Middle East.

Pope Urban II, head of the Catholic Church, believed that Christians had a right to the Holy Land of Jerusalem. He called on knights to take back Jerusalem from the Muslims. Over 4,000 knights answered Pope Urban II's call to fight. In 1096, they began the battle to win back Jerusalem. Their war cry was "God Wills It!"

Fierce and bloody, the First Crusade was also a success. In 1099, the knights captured Jerusalem. They showed no mercy on their conquered enemies, slaughtering the Turks.

Later Crusades

Many other Crusades followed. Control of the Holy Land passed back and forth between

Christians and Muslims. Each Crusade was extremely bloody, causing huge losses of life.

These later Crusades were almost always failures for the European knights. Many crusaders died on the battlefield. Countless others died of disease and hunger. Convinced that God wanted them to have the Holy Land, knights didn't understand why they were losing in battle. They thought of themselves as holy warriors. They believed their faith would always lead them to victory.

Godfrey of Bouillon was one of the leaders of the First Crusade. Godrey, a French knight, helped capture Jerusalem and became the city's first Christian ruler.

Tales from the Middle Ages were often stories of magic and wizardry. Many tales praised knights. The most famous legend combined both knighthood and magic. This was the legend of King Arthur. According to myth, Arthur ruled a land called Camelot. He fought evil with his magic sword, Excalibur.

One story tells that as a boy, Arthur was the only one able to remove Excalibur from the stone in which it was stuck. Arthur was crowned king and married the lovely Guinevere.

King Arthur led a cavalry of twelve knights. These heroic fighters were known as the Knights of the Round Table. Unfortunately, King Arthur was betrayed by the knight whom he trusted most—Sir Lancelot. Lancelot had secretly fallen in love with Queen Guinevere. Once Arthur learned of this secret romance, the Round Table was finished. Without these heroic knights, Arthur's kingdom soon crumbled.

This painting shows another story of how Arthur got Excalibur. In this version, Arthur rows to the Lady of the Lake who will present him with the magical sword.

15

CHAPTER TWO

Living by the Sword

As the value of knights rose, so did the cost of being one. It became harder for knights to afford the armor and fine horses they needed in battle. These items were too costly for a poor peasant to buy. By the eleventh century, most knights were wealthy noblemen.

A Lifelong Pursuit

Knighthood was often passed down from father to son. Future knights might begin their training at the age of four. These young boys were taught how to ride ponies. A few years later, they would be given positions as pages.

This Scottish sword, which dates to the 1600s, is almost 5 feet long (1.5 meters). Because of its length and weight, a knight needed to use both hands to swing the sword in battle.

A page served the lord of the castle, performing errands. During their free time, pages learned to hunt animals with a spear and a bow. Using blunt, wooden swords, they sharpened their skills for future battles. They also used small round shields called bucklers.

At fourteen, a talented page was promoted to squire. Each squire assisted one knight. Squires performed all kinds of chores, from serving meals to cleaning swords. Squires followed knights everywhere—even on the battlefield. If a knight lost a weapon while in battle, his squire rushed into combat to replace it.

After learning these skills, squires were knighted. Squires stayed up the night before their knighting ceremonies. They prayed until morning in a church, refusing to eat or sleep. At dawn, they took a long bath and dressed in a white linen robe. At the ceremony, a squire swore to use his sword only for God. His lord

These knight and horse armors date to about 1575. Under his armor, a knight usually wore a linen shirt and underpants, a shirt with chain-mail padding on the arms and chest, and a chain-mail neck collar.

tapped the flat edge of a sword against the squire. At this point, the squire was dubbed, or knighted.

Dressed to Kill

Because knights fought in close quarters, they covered themselves from head to toe in armor. However, the helmets knights wore made their heads extremely hot. So they carried their helmets until the battle began.

FIGHTING WORDS

A single suit of armor could take three years to make.

Knights also wore a short tunic called a hauberk. Hauberks were made of chain mail and draped over the neck. Chain mail was made of up to forty thousand tiny links of metal. Hauberks protected knights from having their necks slashed open by enemy swords. By the late Middle Ages, knights began wearing a plate of armor over the chain mail. Armor plates prevented arrows from piercing the knights' bodies.

These metal lance points were designed to pierce the armor of an opposing knight. Medieval lances could measure up to 19 to 23 feet (6 to 7 meters) long.

Tools of Battle

Besides wearing protective chain mail, knights also relied on several weapons to conquer enemies. Each knight carried a kite-shaped shield in his left hand, while holding his sword in the right. At the start of the Middle Ages, knights used double-edged swords and slashed at their foes. Later on, the sword was built to be stronger and stiffer. A new diamond-shaped tip allowed knights to stab victims through their links of chain mail. Knights also used axes, daggers, and falchions. A falchion is a weapon that looked like a butcher's cleaver.

The warhorses that knights rode into battle were well trained. The horses, called destriers, were bred for combat. To attack his enemy,

a knight raised himself up on his warhorse, almost to a standing position. He held his lance beside him. Then the warhorse galloped toward his enemy. Both knight and horse turned into a kind of living missile. While charging, the knight tried to stab the enemy to death with his lance.

Tournaments

During peacetime, knights competed in tournaments to keep their battle skills sharp. During tournaments, knights treated each other as if they were enemies. People traveled from far and wide to watch these events.

Until about 1200, tournaments often took the form of a melee. This meant that knights actually fought one another in hand-to-hand combat. In these mock battles, they even took one another hostage. While melees thrilled tournament spectators, they were very dangerous to the warriors. The fierce fighting often got out of hand, leading to injuries and even deaths. Rules were made to make the events safer. Tournament judges limited the places where knights could hit each other with their weapons.

Tournaments also featured a wildly popular event called jousting. In a joust, knights charged one another on horseback, carrying lances. The victorious knight had to be skilled with his horse. He also had to bravely withstand the impact of the other knight's lance. Most jousts were peaceful. The dueling warriors

In this photo, actors dress as sixteenth-century knights and take part in a joust.

used blunted weapons. During war jousts, knights fought with sharpened swords and lances—and the events could end in tragedy. When the church learned how many knights were dying at tournaments, they tried to ban them. The contests were far too popular, though, and continued on.

Heraldry

On the battlefield, it was difficult for knights to recognize each other. After all, they were wearing armor that completely covered their faces! A system called heraldry fixed this problem. Heraldry was a practice in which a knight placed a pattern or design on his shield. Each noble family had a basic pattern and set of colors. A family's eldest son inherited the design, called a coat of arms. The other sons would use the same coat of arms, but make it slightly different.

FIGHTING WORDS

If a man married into a rich family, he might add his wife's coat of arms to his own.

24

Chivalry Lives

Knights lived by a certain code. The code demanded that they defend the weak and live an honorable life. Part of the code included chivalry. Chivalry is a type of polite and noble behavior, shown especially toward women. During medieval times, chivalry became a very romantic ideal. Once a knight fell in love with a woman, he worshiped her in the name of chivalry. He dedicated his battles to her. In return, she praised his courage.

Sometimes a woman would give her knight an item of clothing, like a scarf, to wear near his heart while he fought his enemies. The church did not approve of this kind of behavior. In its opinion, women would distract knights from their duty to defend the church. This was another time when the church's rule failed to influence knights. Chivalry did not fade.

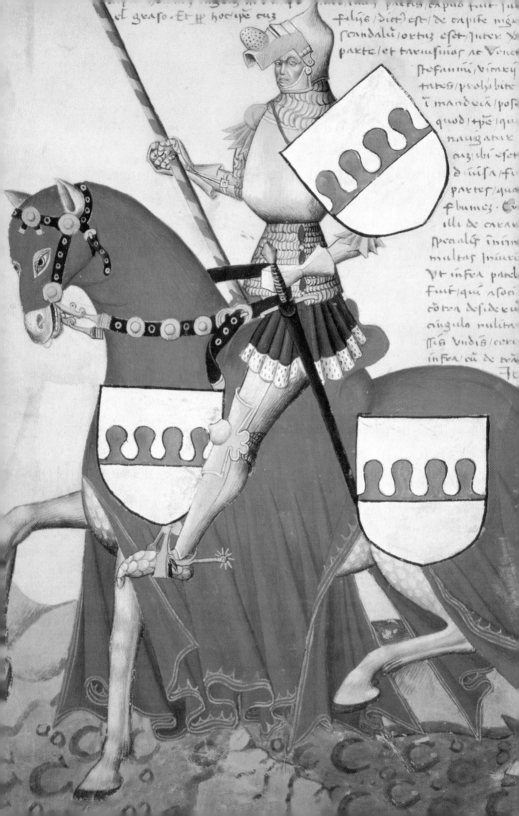

CHAPTER THREE

The Cavalry in Combat

To break enemy ranks, knights on horseback lined up and charged all at once. This tactic was known as the conrois. Because the cavalry could not turn around or back up, they only had one chance to knock out their opponent. Galloping on their horses, with their lances pointed at the enemy, they charged ahead.

Lances weren't the only weapons knights used while charging on their destriers. They also slashed through their enemies' chain mail with swords. While it wasn't easy to control the swords, large knobs at the end of the

This illustration from the fifteenth century shows a knight in armor riding his destrier, or warhorse.

sword's handle, called pommels, helped. Pommels kept the swords balanced, allowing knights to control their swords as they slashed at flesh and metal.

Knights also struck their enemies with heavy maces. A mace was a heavy club with a spike-metal head. Maces were every bit as deadly as swords and lances. Knights swung maces like baseball bats, brutally clubbing their enemies. A well-placed blow could split a foe's skull and crush his bones.

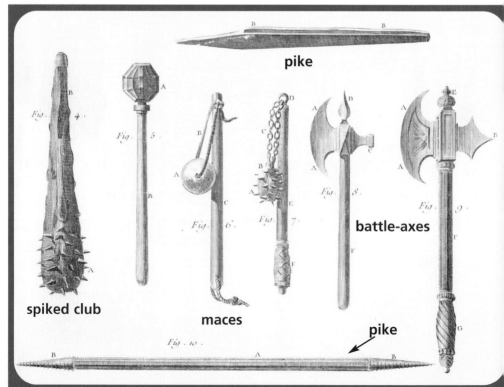

pike

spiked club

maces

battle-axes

pike

On the Defense

FIGHTING WORDS
Some battles were bloodier than others. In some cases, the cavalry would run low on knights. Squires would dash in with swords of their own during these emergencies.

Often during the Middle Ages, invaders tried to take over castles. Knights protecting the castle charged the invaders before they reached the castle gates. The knights often took some invaders hostage and killed the others.

However, it wasn't always possible for knights to beat invaders to the punch. Sometimes, the invaders managed to surround a castle. When this happened, residents had to make sure their castle was well stocked with food. That's because the enemy often remained outside the castle for days, even months. They hoped to starve the knights and lords to death. Some attackers even dug under a castle's walls to get inside.

Knights carried a fearsome assortment of deadly weapons into battle.

The Battle of Antioch

In October 1097, during the First Crusade, the cavalry marched toward Antioch, the "city of great towers." Antioch was an important city in the area around the Mediterranean Sea. As long as the Turks controlled it, Christians could not peacefully travel to the Holy Land of Jerusalem.

The crusaders began their invasion sure they could capture Antioch quickly. The battle, however, was fiercer than they had imagined. The knights could not break through Antioch's walls. Some knights found their will weakening. A few began to desert the scene. Those who stayed were dying of hunger and disease.

Seven months into the battle, the tide finally turned. On June 3, 1098, a Turkish soldier betrayed his people when he let crusaders scale a wall and enter the city.

The conquest of Antioch by the crusaders in 1098 was an important battle in the First Crusade. After capturing Antioch, the crusaders moved on to Jerusalem where they claimed final victory in July 1099.

Once inside, the knights quickly drew their swords and began fighting. By the end of June, those Turks who were not dead had fled Antioch.

This statue of Richard the Lionhearted stands in London, England. Richard fought against the French and was killed in battle by an arrow in 1199.

The Crusades Continue

The Third Crusade made a hero out of England's Richard the Lionhearted. Though Richard lost the Crusade, he signed an important treaty with the Turks in 1192. The treaty won Christians the right to continue pilgrimages to the Holy Land.

The Crusades continued for two hundred years. Control over the Holy Land shifted back and forth until 1244. At that point, Muslims took control of Jerusalem for the final time. By the end of the thirteenth century, the crusading Christians and knights had been driven out of the area. In all, there were eight Crusades. Each began for a different reason. However, each ended with the same result—bloodshed and loss of life.

Help From the Enemy

Medieval warfare took a gruesome toll on a knight's body. In their armor, crusaders sweltered in the Middle East's desert climate. Others suffered from hunger and disease. Knights didn't have doctors to help them or hospitals in which to recover. Europeans knew very little about medicine. As a result, many knights died of battle wounds.

During the Middle Ages, Muslims knew much more about medicine. At first, knights refused to trust Muslim knowledge. By the fifteenth century, Europeans finally started practicing Muslim ways of healing. Some historians say that this sharing of knowledge was one of the few good things to come from the Crusades.

Orders From God

During the Crusades, many knights joined religious military orders. Knights founded these orders to combine charity, faith, and bravery on the battlefield. Three of the most famous orders were the Templar Knights, the Hospitalers, and the Teutonic Knights.

The Templar Knights were known for their banking skills. They invented a system of depositing money in one town and using it in another. This was an early version of a checking account.

This building in Marienburg, Germany, became the home of the Teutonic Knights in 1309. The building was built in 1272.

The Hospitalers started out with a mission of helping sick pilgrims. Soon they began defending the Holy Land as well. The Teutonic Knights were involved in trade and politics. They converted many people to Christianity.

The Hospitalers and Teutonics are still charitable orders today, helping the sick and those in need. The Templars met a far different fate. By the fourteenth century, rumors spread that the Templars were worshiping the devil. Many Templars were burned at the stake.

CHAPTER FOUR

The Legacy Lives

After the thirteenth century, a knight's role in society became less important. Although they still fought bravely in battle, combat styles were going through drastic changes. During the Hundred Years' War (1337–1453), a new form of fighting overwhelmed the knights' cavalries—archery. Again and again, archers with longbows and crossbows defeated armored knights. Steel-tipped arrows could fly a quarter of a mile and puncture armor. Many knights perished in this long, intense war.

Foot soldiers created another new weapon in the fourteenth century called the halberd.

Our fascination with the times and lifestyle of knights still goes on. This photo is from a historical reenactment at Chilham Castle, in Kent, England. The castle was built in the late 1200s.

These long axes were topped with curved spikes. When knights charged a soldier carrying a halberd, they often met a gruesome end. Their enemy would catch them with the curve of the axe, then split their skulls.

Once gunpowder was introduced to western Europe sometime in the fourteenth century, the knight's era was all but over. Cannons and guns packed far more power than an entire cavalry did. These new weapons not only did more damage than swords and lances, but were also more accurate. Skilled knights were no match for these new ways of warfare.

This man is wearing chain mail and armor scales at a reenactment of the Battle of Hastings, fought in 1066.

The Country Gentleman

Knights began living on big estates rather than at the king's castle. Many preferred living the life of a gentleman to fighting wars. Wealthy knights often paid artists and poets to create works for them.

The knights' wealthy lifestyle soon became harder to maintain. Merchants and farmers were making more money than knights. Nobles no longer took to the battlefield. Peasants did the fighting instead. Knights steadily lost their influence with kings. Yet by the fifteenth century, chivalry was still embraced. It now had little to do with battlefield bravery. It was now more an ideal of how to behave in public. People displayed suits of armor for show, not battle.

FIGHTING WORDS

Charles VII of France formed Europe's first professional army in 1415. He saw his cavalry cornered and killed by archers at the battle of Agincourt and realized that the days of the knights were over.

39

Gone, but Not Forgotten

In recent years, groups have tried to bring medieval history back to life. People dress up in chain mail. They carry weapons once used by knights. They hold jousting events, tournaments, and more. These groups perform for delighted audiences across the world.

For many years, films, TV programs, and books have captured the magic of chivalry and knighthood. These works of art entertain and delight audiences and readers. They also inform people about the myths and legends of chivalry.

Honorary Knighthood

The code of chivalry that knights stood for is still honored. Each year, the Queen of England chooses people who have made a great impact on society to receive the title of knighthood. Politicians, surgeons, and entertainers have won the honor. Steven Spielberg, former New

At this jousting tournament in Florida, spectators get a close-up look at two knights charging one another on their destriers.

York City mayor Rudolph Giuliani, and soccer star Pelé have all been granted knighthood status. Honored women receive the title of Dame.

Knights haven't seen a battlefield in centuries. Their days of warfare, Crusades, and melees are long over. Yet people continue to cherish the ideals of knighthood. Many men and women are still amazed by the myths and history of the Middle Ages.

New Words

cavalry (**kav**-uhl-ree) soldiers who fight on horseback

chain mail (**chayn mayl**) flexible armor made of many metal rings linked together

chivalry (**shiv**-uhl-ree) a code of noble and polite behavior that was expected of a medieval knight

conrois (**cuhn**-wa) a battle tactic where the entire cavalry charged the enemy at once

crossbow (**krawss**-boh) a weapon with a bow mounted across a piece of wood

Crusades (Kroo-**saydz**) battles fought in the eleventh, twelfth, and thirteenth centuries by European Christians attempting to capture biblical lands from the Muslims

destrier (**dess**-tree-ay) a knight's steed, or warhorse

New Words

feudalism (**fyoo**-duh-li-zuhm) the medieval system in which people were given land and protection by the owner of the land, or lord, and in return worked and fought for him

jousting (**joust**-ing) a battle between two knights riding horses and armed with lances

longbow (**lawng**-boh) a hand-drawn wooden bow held vertically

melee (**may**-lay) a hand-to-hand fight among several people

pages (**pay**-jes) a knight's boy servant

pilgrimage (**pil**-gruhm-edj) a journey to worship at a holy place

squire (**skwire**) a young nobleman who helped a knight and accompanied him into battle

For Further Reading

Corrick, James. *Life of a Medieval Knight.* Farmington Hills, MI: Lucent Books, 2001.

Hilliam, Paul. *Weapons and Warfare: Armies and Combat in Medieval Times.* New York: Rosen Publishing Group, Inc., 2003.

Oakeshott, R. Ewart. *A Knight and His Armor.* Chester Springs, PA: Dufour Editions, Inc., 1999.

Wolfson, Evelyn. *King Arthur and His Knights in Mythology.* Berkeley Heights, NJ: Enslow Publishers, Inc., 2002.

Resources

Organizations

Medieval Institute
715 Hesburgh Library
University of Notre Dame
Notre Dame, IN 46556
(574) 631-6603
www.nd.edu/%7emedinst/

Medieval Academy of America
104 Mount Auburn Street, 5th floor
Cambridge, MA 02138
(617) 491-1622
www.medievalacademy.org

The Center for Medieval Studies, Inc.
PO Box 4688
Salinas, CA 93912
(831) 443-6451
www2.medievalstudies.org/ms/

RESOURCES

Web Sites

Enter the Middle Ages
http://www.mnsu.edu/emuseum/history/
middleages/
Take a virtual tour of the days of chivalry on this
Web site. Get your information from one of four
different "tour guides": a peasant, a nun, a
merchant, or, of course, a knight!

Exhibits Collection—The Middle Ages
www.learner.org/exhibits/middleages/
Want to know what it was really like to live in
the Middle Ages? This Web site gives you the
facts—from what clothing people wore to what
they did for fun.

Discovery Channel—Making of a Knight
http://dsc.discovery.com/convergence/
tournament/tournament.html
This Web site is filled with features about
tournaments, warfare, and plagues. Of course,
there's also a quiz about love. Take it to see if
you're a fan of chivalry or not.

Index

Index

About the Author

Aileen Weintraub is an author and editor living in upstate New York. She has published over thirty-five books for children and young adults.